AF886562

Attorney Barry Feinstein For Over 25 Years Fighting The Big Insurance Companies

ISBN: 978-1-946481-03-0

Designed and Published by:

Speakeasy Publications

73-03 Bell Blvd, #10

Oakland Gardens, NY 11364

www.SpeakeasyMarketingInc.com

888-225-8594

DISCLAIMER

This publication is intended to be informational only. No legal advice is being given, and no attorney-client relationship is intended to be created by reading this material. If you are facing legal issues, whether criminal or civil, seek professional legal counsel to get your questions answered.

Law Offices of Barry Feinstein & Affiliates, P.C.
100 Lowell Street,
Peabody, MA 01960
(978) 531-7450
www.barryfeinstein.com

TESTIMONIALS

"I had a rather serious slip and fall accident and broke my shoulder. It never occurred to me to hire a lawyer to represent me with this issue until some of my friends started telling me that I should. I researched some local personal injury law firms and decided on Barry Feinstein and Affiliates. From the very first meeting, I was impressed with Attorney Feinstein and his team, especially Tracy. I provided them with all the paperwork and information I had and they took it from there and did their own research. They made a difficult situation very easy by preparing all the documents and only called me when they needed additional specific information. I asked Attorney Feinstein how long he thought it would take to complete the case and he said about 1-1 1/2 years. In fact, he completed the case and presented me with a very nice offer in 1 year. I would recommend Barry Feinstein & Affiliates to anyone seeking a personal injury lawyer."

- *Elizabeth K.*

****

"After a tragic event there is no greater peace of mind than justice being served. To receive justice and be awarded a stepping stone to get life back onto a better path for my family and I have given me more gratitude than I can express to Attorney Barry Feinstein and staff! They've been exceptionally wonderful handling my case with care and compassion, informing and explaining everything to me every step of the way. I am very pleased I made the call to attorney Feinstein for help and would recommend him to everyone!!!"

- *Kelly M.*

****

"Attorney Feinstein has helped me three times over a 20 year span. Each time I was more impressed than the last. From my first meeting with him I knew I was being represented by the figurative "pit bull". His staff is the best. They are right there and ready to assist in any way possible. My phone calls are returned and my questions answered in a timely and professional manner. From the moment I hired him to the moment it was over I was treated and felt like the most important client he had. Attorney Barry got me my out of pocket expenses for medications, lost wages from missing work and he was able to settle my case not only for better money than I would have ever expected, but so much quicker than I could have hoped for. If you get into an accident and you don't hire Attorney Feinstein, you don't have the best lawyer in the business. I refer my family and friends without hesitation."

- A Client

****

"I was involved in a car accident where I was rear ended. I attempted to work with the insurance company myself and got overwhelmed. I called Attorney Feinstein's office. I took the pile of papers I had to them and was assured they would help me. To my amazement, they made everything so smooth. In the end, I was very pleased with the agreements that were hashed out between the insurance company and them. It was so seamless. I didn't feel any pressure. I was treated far superior than I expected during that whole mess! If you want an attorney who cares and will do the best FOR YOU. This is your man!!"

- Chrissy D.

****

"Barry and his team were very professional and helpful while working with me on my case. He took the time to go over everything with me and made sure I knew what was going on. They always responded to my phone calls and emails in a prompt and friendly manner and answered any questions that I had. He took all of the stress out of the situation and made the process much easier to deal with. I would recommend Barry Feinstein and Affiliates to anyone looking for a hardworking, professional lawyer to help with your case."

- Matt S.

****

"When I was injured at the workplace, I called Barry Feinstein and he saw me in his office the next day. All though he does not personally deal with Worker's Comp, he referred me to an associate who does. Worker's Comp is impossible to navigate without professional help, and thanks to Barry and his team, I had a favorable outcome. If you are ever injured at work or otherwise, call Barry Feinstein immediately. He can help. Thanks Barry!"

- Steve K.

****

TABLE OF CONTENTS

AUTHOR INTRODUCTION

Barry A. Feinstein graduated from Northeastern University in 1973, and New England School of Law in 1977. He is licensed to practice in the Commonwealth of Massachusetts, United States District Court of Massachusetts, and the United States Supreme Court. He is a sustaining member of the American Association for Justice. He is also a member of the American Bar Association, Massachusetts Academy of Trial Attorneys and Massachusetts Bar Association. Finally, Attorney Feinstein is also the past President of the Peabody Bar Association.

His areas of practice are Litigation & Appeals, Medical Malpractice, Motor Vehicle Accidents — Plaintiff, Nursing Home, Personal Injury — Plaintiff, Products Liability Law, Professional Malpractice Law, Sexual Harassment, Social Security — Disability, Toxic Torts, and Workers' Compensation Law.

BAR ADMISSIONS

1) Massachusetts

EDUCATION

1) J.D., New England School of Law, Boston, Massachusetts, 1977
2) B.A., Northeastern University, Boston, Massachusetts, 1973

PROFESSIONAL ASSOCIATIONS AND MEMBERSHIPS

1) American Association for Justice, *Sustaining Member*

2) Massachusetts Academy of Trial Attorneys, *Member*

3) Massachusetts Bar Association, *Member*

4) American Bar Association, *Member*

5) Peabody Bar Association, *Past President*

BIRTH INFORMATION

October 21, 1951, Boston, Massachusetts, United States of America

How Has Your Experience Been In Handling Personal Injury Cases?

I've been concentrating my practice in personal injury law for over 25 years. I find it to be quite rewarding. People come in and unfortunately, they are injured or they are hurt. We try to help get the medical bills paid, and we try to get their lost wages reimbursed; hopefully when they are feeling better, which most are only when we reach a result where the doctor says "this is the best that you are going to be," then most times we are able to provide them with a significant check. That doesn't take the pain away but under our system of laws, that is an attempt to try and make them whole after an accident. So I find that quite rewarding that we can take that pressure off the people in terms of getting medical bills taken care of and getting their lost wages reimbursed, and helping to get them compensated at the end.

What Makes Your Firm Particularly Suited To Handle Personal Injury Cases?

The fact that we've been fighting the big insurance companies for over 25 years makes us particularly suited to handle personal injury claims. During that period of time, we've utilized those systems to streamline the process. We make it a point to stay in contact and communicate with our clients on a continued basis and we make every attempt to maximize the amount of monies they receive in a timely manner.

Can Someone Even Afford An Experienced Personal Injury Attorney?

Yes. Most cases are taken on what is called a contingency basis. We are paid on a percentage of the recovery. The client doesn't have to provide a retainer. By that, I mean that the client doesn't have to provide a check or monies upfront.

Misconceptions About Personal Injury Attorneys And The Recovery Process

Many people have a misconception that the process can take many years when in fact, with many smaller cases, a claim might be resolved within 9 months to 12 months. Some of the more significant cases can take a year and a half to two years. I'm not saying that's always the case, but many people have a misconception that this is going to take 4, 5 or 7 years. Because this is all that we do and this is all that we've been doing for a long period of time, we utilize systems that have streamlined the process. As I said, the smaller cases, we are able to resolve many of them in as little as 9-12 months.

Statute Of Limitations For Bringing A Personal Injury Lawsuit In Massachusetts

The Massachusetts statute of limitations is 3 years for personal injury cases and it's 4 years for cases involving workers' compensation. I would note though that there are also certain notice requirements. So they could be as short as 30 days for a defect in a public way, or they could be two years in a claim against cities and states. Each case is individual and we have to look at each case for the statute against the notice requirements.

Exception For Minors In The Statute Of Limitations

In Massachusetts, a minor child must file a medical malpractice lawsuit within three years from the date the minor's parents had knowledge or sufficient notice that the defendant's medical treatment may have caused the child's injuries, with one exception: a minor child less than six years old has until his/her ninth birthday to file a medical malpractice lawsuit.

Do Most Personal Injury Claims Settle Prior To Trial?

Most cases do end up settling at some point. They can either settle within that 9 to 12 month window and there are other cases that settle before the trial or that settle while the jury is still making their decision. Every case that comes into our office is prepared for a trial. If you are going to settle a case, you must be sure to settle the case fairly and get people the compensation that they deserve. It has to be done from a position of strength, and so we don't accept the case to settle it. When we accept a case, we prepare that case like it's going to be tried.

How Soon Should You Seek Medical Treatment After Sustaining An injury?

When you think you should receive medical treatment is certainly a decision for the client to make. Your course of treatment should be decided between the client and

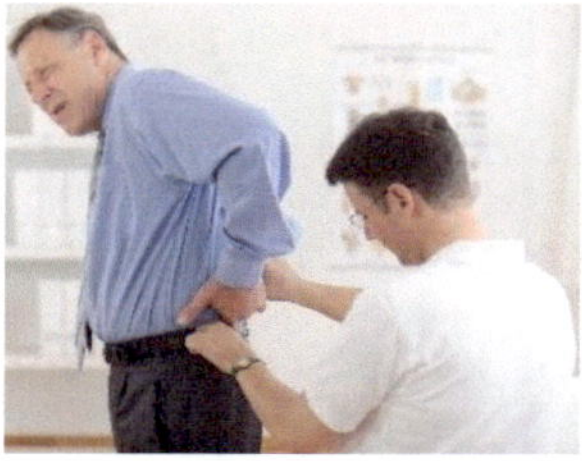

their doctor. I would recommend that if somebody has an injury, that they seek medical treatment as soon as possible. If they wait too long, the argument could be made that the injury wasn't as severe as it could have been or maybe it was some other incident that caused or contributed to the injury.

Importance Of Following Doctor's Advice In A Personal Injury Case

When you have gaps in medical treatment, there is the argument that the injury isn't as severe as it could have been. If there are gaps in treatment or if you miss a lot of doctor's appointments, then one could argue that the injury just isn't as serious as it could have been.

How Does Fault Or No-Fault State Apply To An Auto Accident Claim?

Massachusetts is a no-fault state. What that means is there are what's called PIP benefits and that applies to automobile accidents. If you have this coverage, and most people do (although some people waive the coverage in an attempt to lower their insurance costs), then no matter who is deemed at fault, their insurance company will pay the first $2000 in medical bills, then it goes to the health insurance carrier if they have health insurance. If the health insurance doesn't cover that particular form of treatment, the PIP carrier will pay up to $8000 in medical bills and/or lost wages regardless of who is deemed to be at fault. If the other party is deemed to be at fault then that insurance company will collect whatever they paid from the other party's insurance company. It's a little bit of a complicated system and that's why it is a good idea to have an attorney help you.

Am I Required To Notify My Own Insurance Company Once An Accident Has Occurred?

Yes, it is advisable to notify your own insurance company once an accident has occurred as soon as possible.

Am I Responsible For Notifying The Other Driver's Insurance Company Of The Accident?

If you hire our law firm, we'll take care of notifying the other driver's insurance company of the accident for you.

How Important Are Evidence And Witnesses In Auto Accident Cases?

Evidence and witnesses are very important in any personal injury claim. If there is a dispute as to who is responsible for the accident, evidence and witnesses are vital. With the advance of technology, it's important for clients to utilize their smartphones to photograph the evidence, the locus of the accident, tire tracks, skid marks, and pictures of the point of impact.

How Serious Are Injuries Sustained In Motorcycle Accidents?

The types of injuries that we see in motorcycle accidents are oftentimes more serious. Common sense would dictate that in cases involving motorcycle accidents, there is nothing between the operator of the motorcycle and the road. So when you are comparing a motorcycle accident to a car accident, in cars there is metal between the driver and the point of impact. The physics of the motorcycle accident often has the driver being thrown over the handlebars and that can provide a very serious injury.

Is A Motorcycle Driver Or Passenger Required To Wear A Helmet And Safety Gear In Massachusetts?

Yes, a helmet is required when operating or riding on a motorcycle. If someone is not wearing a helmet, I would think that it would be a factor in ascribing some sort of comparative negligence upon the operator if they fail to comply with the law on wearing a helmet.

Could Not Wearing A Helmet Affect The Value Of My Accident Claim?

Yes, not wearing a helmet can affect the value on an accident claim. Specifically, if the other party is deemed to be at fault and you weren't wearing a helmet, it may possibly reduce your award by a certain percentage based on the fact that you were not wearing a helmet. The theory here is that if you were wearing a helmet, then maybe the injury would not have been as severe.

What Do You Look For In A Viable Motorcycle Accident Case?

In a viable motorcycle accident case, I'm specifically looking to see if the fault is on the other operator.

Importance Of Hiring An Attorney Experienced In Specifically Handling Motorcycle Accident Cases

An attorney who is experienced in handling motorcycle accident cases would be an individual who is experienced in the nuances involved in motorcycle riding. Further, the recognizance of blind spots which may exist in the locus of the accident and be aware of the vulnerability of the driver of the motorcycle. Motorcycle riding is very popular in Massachusetts and throughout the nation, and of particular importance is the fact that a lot of Massachusetts' roads are narrow. They are winding and there are blind spots. This is why somebody should be experienced in handling motorcycle cases and be aware of the locus of where the incident occurred.

Common Causes Of Commercial Vehicle Accidents

Common causes of commercial vehicles accidents are driver errors, faulty equipment, fatigue, and the driver not paying attention to the road.

Types Of Commercial Vehicles We Are Referring To

We are talking about large truck accidents.

Injuries Resulting From Commercial Vehicle Accidents

Cases that our office or our affiliate offices have been involved in would involve brain injuries, various back, neck, arm, and leg injuries with a hardware inserted. By that I mean large plates and pins.

What Kind Of Evidence Is Important To Preserve And Collect In Commercial Vehicle Wrecks?

It's imperative that as soon as possible, documentary evidence is assembled and prepared. Photographs of the scene are very essential. In some cases an accident reconstruction expert may be brought out to reconstruct the locus and entire area of the accident.

Who Can Be Held Liable For A Commercial Vehicle Accident?

The operator, the owner, the trucking company, the company that the vehicle was carrying the product for, and the company that loaded the vehicle, among others may all be held liable for a commercial vehicle accident.

Are There Any Special Rules Of The Road Regarding Bicyclists?

Bicyclists must refrain from negligent operation of their bicycle. They should follow the rules of the roads where they are riding, obey traffic signals

and stop lights, drive in the same direction as traffic, use hand signals when turning, and opertate in bicycle lanes, if applicable. We are looking at Massachusetts roads which are narrow and there are blind spots. The injury that occurs to bicyclists are often times very serious because again, there is nothing between the bicyclist and the road.

Determining Viability Of A Bicycle Accident Claim

I determine the viability of a bicycle accident claim by looking at driver error, and then looking at how careful a bicyclist was. Both of those are complimentary elements.

Comparative Fault When It Comes To Bicycle Accidents

Yes, there is comparative fault when it comes to bicycle accidents. If an individual does not follow the rules of the road, or is not wearing a helmet, this could minimize the damages.

An Example Of Someone Who Has Contributed To Their Own Bicycle Accident

An example of someone who might have contributed to their own bicycle accident could be, a person was riding in the middle of the road where there were cars, they were veering in between cars and going back and forth. They weren't staying within a bicycle lane. Those would be several possibilities among many.

Do Most Bicycle Injury Cases Reach A Settlement Before Trial?

Most do settle, but again, every case that we take is prepared like it is going to trial. So if a case is going to be settled, it's settled from a position of strength. However, just because most cases are settled, it doesn't necessarily mean that any given case is going to be settled.

Accidents And Injuries Caused In Premises Liability Cases

Premises cases usually involve fall down cases, cases involving flights of stairs, and so forth.

How Do I Know I Have A Premises Liability Claim That Should Be Pursued?

The owner of the premises has to keep their premises in a safe manner. If somebody is injured on somebody's premises and they were caused to be injured because maybe the steps fell apart, maybe a railing on the porch let go, maybe they were walking on the steps and a railing let go, maybe they were walking on the walkway and there was an uneven surface or we can get into cases involving snow and ice when an area wasn't sanded and salted, then those are all areas where the landlord or the property owner would be held responsible.

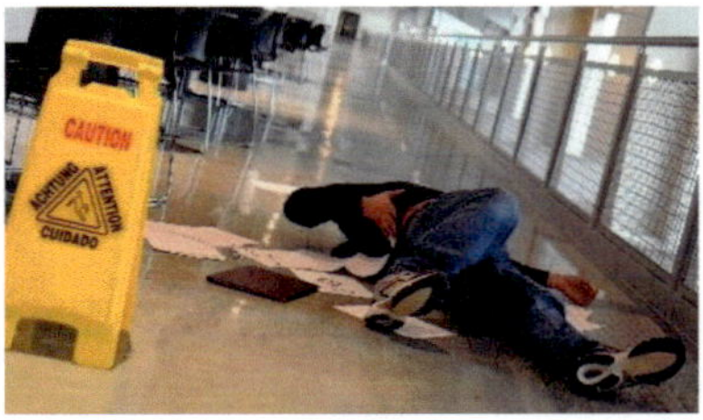

Comparative Fault In Premises Liability Cases

Often times, there is comparative fault in premise liability cases. The person "should have known" or "should have been more careful." So oftentimes, if the walkway was uneven and the injury was serious, there very well may be either a settlement or a verdict and then that might be reduced by a certain percentage because the person either knew or should have known about it and should have been a bit more careful.

Statute Of Limitations For A Premises Liability Claim

There is a 3 year statute of limitations for a premises liability claim.

Conditions That Cause Slip & Fall, Trip & Fall Accidents

We can look at a torn carpet, we can look at poor lighting, we can look at a narrow staircase, we can look at poor drainage, we can look at risers on steps that don't meet building codes, or we can look at breaks in coloration which may provide for an optical illusion (i.e., if all the steps are the same color as the landing, then that may provide an optical illusion). At that point there may be a human factors expert that may be looking to assist us in giving an opinion as to whether there was negligence on part of the owner. We may be talking about treads at the end of steps that may help stop fall down cases on steps.

What Factors Must Be Present For A Viable Slip And Fall Case On A Commercial Property?

Ordinary negligence must be present for a viable slip and fall case on commercial property. It is important to inspect the locus of the fall in the matter of stairs. As I said,

we are talking about risers, breaks in coloration, or treads on the stairs. Relative to commercial properties, if there is a slip and fall involving snow and ice, it's important to look at the locus for the configuration of the property to see if there are ruts or there are areas to allow for a collection of water which then can be allowed to freeze. It's also important to take a look at gutters and drain spouts which allow water to collect and then to freeze.

Who Can Be Held Liable For A Slip And Fall Or A Trip And Fall On A Commercial Property?

The owner of the property can be held liable or the store owner on the property can be held liable. If there is a contractor who did some work improperly; among others in snow and ice cases, the company that does the sanding and the salting may also be responsible.

How Severe Must A Dog Bite Or Injury Be To Make A Claim?

Any dog bite is severe and you can make a claim if you are bitten by a dog. If it's a dog bite that involves one visit to hospital and it might be on a man's arm or leg and if the bite heals

and there is no scar, that would not be as large as a dog bite on a young girl's face which involves one or two visits to a doctor and may have to go to a plastic surgeon and involve some permanent scarring. In both cases, there are claims to be made.

Is Comparative Negligence Possible In Dog Bite Claims?

Comparative negligence is not applicable in dog bite claims in terms of the owner or the keeper of the dog because again, we are not getting into negligence. It's strict liability. So you just have to prove that the bite occurred. When it comes to the keeper of that dog, then it may come into play.

Who Is Held Liable In Dog Bite Injury Claims?

The owner or the keeper of the dog is held strictly liable in dog bite injury claims. By that I mean, you don't have to prove that the owner or keeper of the dog is negligent. All you have to do is to show that the dog bit the client. In some cases, the property owner may also be liable if the property owner knew or should have known that the dog had violent propensities.

Who Pays Damages To Dog Bite Victims?

If there is homeowner's insurance, the homeowner's insurance carrier would pay the damages to the dog bite victim in these claims. If there isn't homeowner's insurance, then it would be the owner of the dog or the keeper of the dog.

How Is Liability Generally Caused In A Medical Malpractice Claim?

Liability is generally caused in a medical malpractice claim when doctors or medical personnel deviate from an acceptable standard of care.

Are There Any Caps For Medical Malpractice Awards In Massachusetts?

No, there are no caps for medical malpractice awards in Massachusetts.

How Long Does A Person Have To File A Medical Malpractice Claim In Massachusetts?

In Massachusetts, a minor child must file a medical malpractice lawsuit within three years from the date the minor's parents had knowledge or sufficient notice that the defendant's medical treatment may have caused the child's injuries, with one exception: a minor child less than six years old has until his/her ninth birthday to file a medical malpractice lawsuit.

If Someone Signs A Consent Form For A Medical Procedure, Do They Still Have A Malpractice Claim?

There are a couple of issues surrounding that. Signing a consent form doesn't void out a client's negligence. What the consent form may do is just limit the responsibility of the doctor for what he says you are consenting to. If he or she goes beyond that point, then they can be sued for negligence. Then the next issue is whether you knew and understood what the consent form was. That's another issue and if you knew and you understood it, then that's a separate issue which could have to be raised.

Who Can Bring A Wrongful Death Suit?

It's the estate that brings the claim in a wrongful death suit.

What Economic Damages Are Survivors Entitled To In A Wrongful Death Claim?

The economic damages would be predicated upon the age and the work history of the deceased. By that I mean if the deceased was young or middle aged, you can look at what his wages would have been for that period of time that he or she

would have lived. You'd look at what the medical bills were and then you'd look at the pain and suffering.

Are Punitive Damages Recoverable In Such Cases?

Punitive damages may be recoverable in wrongful death cases.

How Are Damages Divided In A Wrongful Death Case Which Involves Multiple Heirs To The Deceased?

If there was a will, then the damages would be divided in accordance with the will. If there wasn't a will, then the damages would go according to bloodline.

Statute Of Limitations For A Wrongful Death Claim

The statute of limitations for filing a wrongful death claim is 3 years.

Injuries Sustained In Nursing Home Abuse Cases

It can go from deviation from a standard of care. There can be serious injuries when the bed rails aren't put up. Often times there can be serious injuries involved and bed sores. There can be serious injuries regarding respiration, as well.

Who Can Be Held Liable In Nursing Home Abuse Or Neglect Cases?

The administrator of the nursing home, the nursing home itself, the company that owns the nursing home, the doctor who is treating the patient, and staff members, among others, can all be held liable in a nursing home abuse or neglect case.

What Steps Can I Take On Behalf Of A Loved One If I Suspect Nursing Home Abuse Or Neglect?

The first step would be to contact our office and we would take things from there in terms of beginning the investigation and finding evidence relevant to the investigation.

Disclaimer

This publication is intended to be informational only. No legal advice is being given, and no attorney-client relationship is intended to be created by reading this material. If you are facing legal issues, whether criminal or civil, seek professional legal counsel to get your questions answered.

Law Offices of Barry Feinstein & Affiliates, P.C.
100 Lowell Street,
Peabody, MA 01960
(978) 531-7450
www.barryfeinstein.com

Made in the USA
Monee, IL
05 November 2026

67385050R00024